Ax Your Income Tax
(and Adopt the AMT Now!)

by Kirk A. Bonamici, CPA, MST

PITTSBURGH, PENNSYLVANIA 15222

The contents of this work including, but not limited to, the accuracy of events, people, and places depicted; opinions expressed; permission to use previously published materials included; and any advice given or actions advocated are solely the responsibility of the author, who assumes all liability for said work and indemnifies the publisher against any claims stemming from publication of the work.

All Rights Reserved
Copyright © 2007 by Kirk A. Bonamici, CPA, MST
No part of this book may be reproduced or transmitted
in any form or by any means, electronic or mechanical,
including photocopying, recording, or by any information
storage and retrieval system without permission in
writing from the author.

ISBN: 978-0-8059-8965-6
Printed in the United States of America

First Printing

For more information or to order additional books,
please contact:
RoseDog Books
701 Smithfield Street
Third Floor
Pittsburgh, Pennsylvania 15222
U.S.A.
1-800-834-1803
www.rosedogbookstore.com

Contents

Foreword v

The Conceptual Framework 1

The AMT Conspiracy 5

The Last Visionary 9

The Stats Thing 12

Simplicity and Fairness, Part 1 17

Simplicity and Fairness, Part 2 21

It's the Bureaucracy, Dummy! 28

Afterword 31

Acknowledgements 33

Foreword

In an insane world, the sane man must appear insane.

Save taxes by adopting the alternative minimum tax as our system of taxation in this country? That's crazy talk! You probably picked up this book just to get a chance to bash the accountant for such a stupid idea. Well, I applaud you for getting this far.

Maybe you've been impacted by the alternative minimum tax, or AMT, or maybe you've read a bunch of scary newspaper articles or magazine stories about the AMT, or perhaps you've never heard of the AMT, but the ax-wielding reference in the title caught your eye and you decided to check it out. Whatever your reason, my motivation for writing this is simple – it's time to get a dialogue going in mainstream America about what this tax is about, what's wrong with it (and believe me, there's plenty wrong with it), and how it could be changed to become a tax system that could achieve the (lofty) goals of simplicity and fairness.

I'm sure you're shaking your head at that last point. The AMT as simple and fair? The AMT is roundly criticized as being way too complicated and unfair to pretty much everybody. And I'm not here to tell you that that isn't true. But I have an idea, and my hope is that it is a conversation starter. I would readily admit to you that I'm no visionary (of which there have been precious few, in my opinion, over the last thirty years). I'm more of a cynic by nature which means I believe that in order to make this idea a reality, Congress will have to basically pull the wool over America's eyes. But if Congress has a talent, that would certainly be it, and I'll be more than happy to give them a suggestion as to how to do it which will leave America dancing in the streets.

A couple of caveats as we get going together. First, I'm a New Jersey accountant, born and raised, and I've prepared about twenty thousand

1040's in my career, so far. I've thought for years that New Jerseyans have been treated unfairly by the federal tax system, and that is reflected in my commentary and ideas. People in high (income and property) tax states may appreciate this more than those in "middle" America. But so few of them would potentially be affected by my idea that I'll take my chances. Second, I absolutely do not believe that I have a unique perspective on solving our tax system problems (remember, not a visionary), but I do have a perspective, and I'd love to share it with you.

So, let's have at it.

The Conceptual Framework

Over the course of years of being a CPA and tax preparer, I've faced the quandary of how to explain to my clients what the AMT is, how it works, and why they are being caught up in it. Before 2001, when President George W. Bush pushed the third greatest tax reduction package since World War II through Congress, we probably ran into the AMT only a couple of times a week (in my practice, we handle about 250 returns per week from early February to April 15th each year). So when a client was in AMT, you could usually get away with a half-assed answer about how it was so complicated that most normal people couldn't comprehend it. Further, a good number of CPAs working in local firms or on their own not only had trouble explaining AMT, but if it wasn't for their tax software, they wouldn't even know when it applied (Okay, all you CPAs, bash away at that last comment)!

After 2001, with a reduction in regular income tax rates leading to lower taxes in the regular income tax world without a corresponding decrease in AMT tax rates, AMT became an everyday occurrence that demanded not only better analysis but a more understandable explanation for our clients. And while we still rely on our software to do the complex AMT calculations, if we don't know when to expect AMT to affect a client, it's not saying much about us as tax preparers.

I've read the AMT described elsewhere as the "Darth Vader" of taxes. In the past, I would describe the AMT as an evil parallel tax universe (where, hopefully, only our evil soap opera twins would be affected). But these are not explanations, only value judgments. So, let's get unemotional and break the AMT down into its component pieces. To do that, it would be helpful to start with the main principles of income tax law as a whole. These three tenets that follow form the basis of everything that comprises the Internal Revenue Code. After reading them, you are free to question why the Code, itself, has to be eight thousand pages long. But as you'll come to see, the Code is more about the exceptions to the rules than the rules themselves.

Knowing these rules will not only help to answer most of your tax questions, but will also make you fun at cocktail parties when the topic turns to taxes. (Does this ever happen in real life? I don't know as my cocktail party friends are also accountants).

For your consideration, the three rules of tax law:

1. You get taxed on all of your income and gains.

2. You get a deduction for your business expenses and losses.

3. You get NO deduction for your personal expenses and losses.

As you can tell, folks, it's not rocket science we're talking about here. You might also wonder why accountants get paid decent bucks to prepare tax returns. As I said earlier, the Code is more about the exceptions than the rules, and a good preparer is the one who knows those exceptions and uses them to their client's advantage. You may also be wondering why so many things that are personal in nature can be deducted on an individual tax return. I would suggest to you, in most cases, Congress is trying to influence some social policy and dangles the tax deduction out there as your incentive for doing what they want. We only have to consider the big three itemizable deductions: mortgage interest, property taxes, and charity to see what Congress values.

First, they encourage home ownership because it spurs the economy, and second, philanthropy because organized religion in this country is a powerful voting bloc. I know this last part is very cynical, but I think that other cynics and pragmatists out there can agree that politics today is as much about doing something with your position as getting reelected to it when your term expires.

Getting back to the topic at hand, the conceptual framework of the AMT (remember that's what this chapter is about), we need to introduce two more points from the regular income tax world that will form the basis of comparison between regular income taxes and the AMT: personal exemptions and tax rates.

Currently, everyone in America is entitled to a personal exemption (valued at $3,300 for 2006). The more members of your family, the more deductions you're entitled to (think about what Congress is trying to reward there). The big problem with exemptions is the complexity that you can run into when figuring out who's entitled to actually claim them.

As to tax rates, in the regular income tax world, we have a graduated rate structure based on the following percentages: 10%, 15%, 25%, 28%, 33%, and 35%. Further, every year the amount taxed in each bracket changes based on a cost of living factor which expands the amount taxed at the lower rates before you end up being in the higher brackets.

Based on the discussion so far, let's try to get an overall sense of how you calculate your tax in the regular income tax world. First, tell the IRS all your income. Next, claim as much in deductions as you can (thinking about Schedule A, Itemized Deductions, we're generally talking about medical, taxes, interest, charity, and job and miscellaneous other deductions). Now, on to the personal exemptions, figure out who is eligible to be your dependent.

Congratulations, you've arrived at regular taxable income. Using the rate tables in effect for the current year, calculate your regular world income tax.

For those of you who have ever reviewed the first two pages of your 1040, you realize at this point, you're only about a third of the way down page two of the form. But this is where the AMT first rears its ugly head, and since the complexity of the following credit and other taxes sections on the rest of the 1040 is pretty similar in both tax systems, we'll leave that alone for now.

To reconnoiter (quickly), we've just done some pretty complex stuff and in the process have abided by the first two principles of tax law (remember those?), but have blown away the third (no deduction for the personal stuff).

It is at this point that we begin the adventure of determining whether we have to pay the AMT or not. The mechanics of the calculations and the mind-numbing adjustments that can come into play here are what scare most people and what make this system (as it exists today) way too complex. All of the adding stuff back to regular taxable income, subtracting other stuff, calculating the AMT tax, and then finally comparing your result with the regular world income tax to determine which is higher, befuddles and confounds most people.

The AMT, conceptually, is so much simpler than that. Further, it is truer to the three main principles of tax law than the regular income tax code is.

Step by step, let's think of it this way:

1. Tell the IRS all of your income (basically, page one of the 1040, same as the regular income tax).

2. Take deductions for interest (just mortgage interest for most people) and charity.

3. Take a big, fat exemption to cover everything else.

4. Multiply the net result by a flat rate of tax (26% for most people).

There it is. That's all. Can it really be that simple? Well, no, but it could be. The AMT needs a good tweaking to get it where mainstream America can embrace it as "the" system. But now that we understand the simple framework which it is based on, we can begin to consider our "alternatives."

Our starting point will be the conspiracy which drives the AMT from behind the scenes and the man who I believe got us as close to a fair and simple tax system as we've been in the preceding thirty years: the last visionary.

The AMT Conspiracy

I

It was a dark and stormy night.

At 1600 Pennsylvania Avenue (the White House), it was the final days of Lyndon B. Johnson's presidency. Three men were huddled in a dimly lit room deep within the bowels of those hallowed halls of democracy. The fate of the free world was at stake as they grappled with a problem that was creating a furor greater than America's desire to end the Vietnam War.

II

Actually, I have no idea if that ever happened or not. I've always wanted to write a spy thriller, though, so let's conjecture further.

III

The copy of <u>The Washington Post</u> sat on his desk. One hundred copies of the news piece picked up by papers across the country lay strewn across the conference room table with their letters of outrage from the American taxpaying public attached to them. Exactly 155 individuals with incomes over $200,000 paid no federal income taxes for 1967. Twenty of them were millionaires. If something wasn't done soon, a taxpayer revolt could happen and stretch the country's already strained financial resources to the breaking point.

Richard Nixon would soon be taking the oath of office as the country's next president. How could this problem be solved?

IV

I'm always amazed at the psychology of what gets America galvanized. Kind of like the coverage Tom Cruise got when he jumped on Oprah's sofa to proclaim his love for Katie Holmes.

V

"Twenty millionaires are not going to be the focus of my first year in office," the new president proclaimed to the three men he had summoned to the Oval Office.

Treasury Secretary Joseph Barr, Assistant Secretary Stanley Surrey, and Chairman of the House Ways and Means Committee, Wilbur Mills, looked at each other and then back at the President.

"We have a plan," they said in unison.

VI

And thus, the AMT was born. Originally conceived and designed as a measure to get the "super rich" to pay their fair share of taxes, it had a broader appeal to those with a vision of true tax reform.

VII

The aide walked briskly down the corridor and descended a flight of stairs. He had brought today's <u>New York Times</u> as his supervisor had directed. The date was April 22, 1969.

When he reached his superior's office, the aide presented the newspaper, but his superior waved it off. Another copy lay in front of him.

"Did you see the article on the administration's tax reform proposals regarding the alternative minimum tax?" the superior queried.

"Yes," the aide replied, "I think the American people will be happy to know that millionaires will no longer be able to get away without paying income taxes."

"Hmmm…did you get anything else from the article?" the superior countered.

"What do you mean?"

The superior picked up his copy of the <u>New York Times</u> and handed it to his charge. "Read the underlined passage," he directed.

The aide took the paper and read from a message that the Nixon administration had included with its tax reform proposal to Congress, "where we can prevent it by law, we must not permit our wealthiest citizens to be one hundred percent successful at tax avoidance. Nor should the government limit its tax reform only to those relatively few extreme cases."

When the aide finished, he looked at his superior who said, "Do you see now?"

"Sir, they're looking for a tax system that would impact a lot more than just a few millionaires. The American people will never go for that. As complicated as the current system is, most people want to at least feel that the rich are paying more than them, and when it comes to taxes, they don't want to be lumped into the rich group."

The superior looked approvingly at his aide. "The thing about this alternative tax system, though, is that it is ultimately simpler than our current income tax system. It can become "the" tax system, but not today. Psychologically, people are not ready for it. But," and he pondered this thought for a moment, "if we take the long view and try to build it in over a generation, people will be impacted in baby steps with most not realizing that it is their tax system until they are in it. And then it will be too late for them to effectively complain about it."

"But, sir, what about future presidents and Congress? What if they tinker with it or even repeal it before it can truly take hold?"

"Our job and the job of those who will come after us is to make sure that doesn't happen."

VIII

Could it really have happened that way? Are there behind-the-scenes power players who keep the AMT in the Internal Revenue Code as part of a master plan to convert all taxpayers to this system? I'll let you judge for yourself, but consider how few changes the AMT has seen over the last twenty years. Since 1986, other than a few revisions to rates and the exemption amounts (only raised because the complaints of the American people were too much for Congress to bear), the AMT has stayed remarkably similar over the years. During this same stretch of time, the Internal Revenue Code of 1986, as it relates to the regular income tax, has been amended in some way, shape, or form ten times, and in certain respects, retains only a small resemblance to the Code as rewritten by the Tax Reform Act of 1986, when we were as close as we've ever been to having the AMT system become "the" tax system in the United States.

IX

"For fifteen years, sir, we've kept a low profile on the AMT although we do have a lot of people now paying it. Don't you think it's time that we try to make a move with the Internal Revenue Code to bring the two systems into one with more of the features of the AMT?"

The superior sat back in his chair and folded his hands across his chest. "Well, President Reagan's tax cuts have complicated things so much that the American people are clamoring for simplicity in their tax returns. The economy has gotten better in the last few years, and the stock market is racing higher. It might be the right time. But we'll have to put a face on it. Someone the American people respect."

"There is someone who has been talking about tax fairness and simplicity for a few years now. He might be the one."

"Ah, yes," the superior leaned forward in his chair, "Go ahead, make the call. We need to see Senator Bill Bradley."

X

Oh, it could so have happened that way.

The Last Visionary

When you think about the people who have had an influence over your life, they generally fall into two categories: those who positively impact your life and those who negatively impact your life. Our current President George W. Bush would probably get the rap as negatively impacting our lives judging solely by his current popularity numbers (or lack thereof) as I write this book. History may look back on him more kindly when the full affect of the events he has helped put into motion can be truly understood. For now, while we experience these events, it is impossible to know the outcome on ourselves and future generations to make such a determination.

I would throw out for your consideration that a visionary is someone who a majority of the people believe affected their lives in a positive manner and did so on a grand enough scale that they made a difference (real or perceived) on at least a national level. Also, enough time must have passed that their ideas can be considered with a dispassionate eye. People like Nelson Mandela, John F. Kennedy, Franklin Roosevelt, Winston Churchill, and Albert Einstein in the twentieth century would all fit under my definition of visionary.

When it comes to income taxes, something that affects most every American every day (whether we choose to think about it or not), I submit to you another name, Senator Bill Bradley, as the last (tax) visionary.

A graduate of Princeton University and a Rhodes Scholar at Oxford University in England (not to mention a two-time NBA world champion and Pro Basketball Hall of Famer), Bradley was one of the chief architects of the 1986 Tax Reform Act.

According to Citizens for Tax Justice (in Washington, D.C.), the 1986 Tax Reform Act is widely considered to be the best piece of American tax legislation since the adoption of the income tax. Over its first five years, it closed more than $500 billion in loopholes and tax shelters. Among its results:

1. A huge wasteful tax-shelter industry for high-income individuals was shut down.

2. Millions of moderate-income working families received tax relief through a major expansion of the earned income tax credit.

3. Taxes on most families (on average, all but the highest tenth as measured by income) were reduced.

4. The income tax was substantially simplified for most filers.

The Act was highly praised by most economists because it leveled the playing field for businesses and investments, and made our economy more efficient and productive. Let's digest all that for a second and do a little compare and contrast with the AMT.

First, high-income individuals on average paid more under the 1986 Tax Reform Act because tax shelters (can we say, preferences) were not favored in the new law. Under today's AMT, we see a similar result where high incomers pay more due to disallowance of AMT preference items.

Second, moderate-income families paid less in income taxes under the 1986 Act than prior to it. In the AMT, the calculated tax is less than the regular income tax in most cases. Think about this. If 3% of taxpayers paid the alternative minimum tax in 2004, it means that 97% paid the regular income tax because it was more than the AMT.

Third, the 1986 Act reduced tax rates to just two brackets, 15% and 28%. In today's AMT, we have just two brackets, 26% and 28%.

Last, the 1986 Act simplified the tax code for most filers. The AMT (again, conceptually) is simpler than the regular income tax system in today's world.

Of course, some large differences do exist between the 1986 Act and the AMT of today, notably the treatment of capital gains and qualified dividends. In the 1986 Act, there were no preference rates for these items, but in today's AMT, they are tax-advantaged. Why? Because Congress likes you! Stuff like this happens when we, as taxpaying citizens, pick up the phone or write our members of Congress, and tell them what we want. Sometimes, if enough people take up the mantle (or fewer people, but with a lot of clout), Congress does listen and will act.

Well, what do you think? It's not like they're eerily similar, but it is close. Yet, if we were so close to merging these two systems in 1986, how did we get so far apart in 2006? Well, look at George Bush (the first), Bill Clinton, and George Bush (the sequel), and a fractured political process that uses its tax laws to support social goals and special interests. Enough said.

Finally, to Bill Bradley, I say it was a good try, but you were probably ahead of your time. And that's not just because we're both Jersey guys.

The Stats Thing

I know what you're thinking – a chapter with a bunch of statistics on the AMT – BORING!

I encourage you to stick with me here because with just a few statistics, we can lay out the groundwork for the argument as to why and how the AMT should be adopted as the tax system in the United States.

Of course, starting with some recent historical perspective on how the collective minds in Washington, D.C. work, will provide us with a jumping-off point for our AMT analysis. To that end, let's review the 1986 law where the phaseout of itemized deductions for high-income taxpayers was created.

The question is not, "How did they come up with that law?" but rather "How did they get away with passing that law?"

The answer is all about statistics.

When Congress and the White House are looking for more money, it should be no surprise that they look to the path of least resistance. Raising taxes with backdoor tax hikes (finding ways to include previously nontaxable income as taxable or limiting deductions) as opposed to raising tax rates, is historically easier for our federal government to do as it limits the potential number of complainers out there. And for every 100 potential complainers, how many would actually call or write their Congressperson to make their case for why the law should not be passed?

If I suggested it might be only 1 or 2 out of that 100, would you think I'm being too pessimistic about the inertia of the taxpaying public or giving a too optimistic number based on your own notions of the complacency that exists in the country today? Whichever side you choose, feel free to adjust my numbers accordingly.

So, let's take a look at the law that created the phaseout of itemized deductions and what our legislators knew before that revenue raiser was ever put on the table.

First, approximately 70% of all the income tax returns that are filed in this country are done with the taxpayers taking the standard deduction (and thus, not itemizing). This means that 70% of us would not be affected by this law if it was passed. Advantage, Congress.

Next, of the 30% that could be affected, only about 10% would have an income level high enough to actually be impacted by the limitation. Big advantage, Congress.

Finally, of these 10%, only about 2% will take the time to complain about the potential change.

Let us do some math on that with a sample of 1,000 people:

Potential affected people (30%)	300
Actual affected people (10% of 300)	30
Number of expected complainers (2% of 30)	.6 people

Less than one person in 1,000 is anticipated to complain about this tax hike! Game, set, match, Congress.

• • •

Turning our attention back to the AMT, we need to know what Congress knows about the number of people affected by the AMT to get into their heads about why and how they'll change it. Further, once we've considered national statistics (from 2004 tax returns filed), I'll provide you statistics from my NJ-based practice with information culled from our recently completed 2005 tax return filing season.

These national statistics come courtesy of the IRS, the Congressional Budget Office, and the Tax Foundation in Washington, D.C.

For 2004, over 130 million income tax returns were filed with the IRS and of that amount, approximately 3% had an AMT liability calculated greater than the regular income tax liability. Thus, approximately 4 million taxpayers nationwide were impacted by the AMT. But, where these taxpayers are located is important, too (and for this we'll use data from 2003 tax returns filed). Of all returns filed in the country, almost one-third of those impacted came from just nine states and the District of Columbia as shown in the following table:

New Jersey	4.4%
New York	4.2%
Connecticut	3.7%
District of Columbia	3.3%
California	3.1%
Maryland	2.9%
Massachusetts	2.9%
Rhode Island	2.1%
Minnesota	1.9%
<u>Oregon</u>	<u>1.9%</u>
Total	30.4%

With the exception of Minnesota, each of these states (and D.C.) is located on either the East or West Coast, and all impose a state income tax (some also have local income taxes as well).

Okay then, of our 4 million affected taxpayers, 30% are coming from just nine states and D.C. That's 1.2 million taxpayers in (basically) two concentrated blocks with the rest spread all over the country. Assuming the non-concentrated block of taxpayers could not effectively complain loud enough to force change or otherwise impact the AMT, let's focus on the 1.2 million taxpayers who potentially could.

Again, going with our assumption that only 2% of those affected would take the time to complain, we have only 24,000 (1.2 million times 2%) taxpayers attempting to influence Congress on AMT legislation.

And we wonder why Congress doesn't seem to be in any hurry to deal with the AMT issue.

• • •

You're probably wondering why I'm in such a hurry then to get a dialogue going about the AMT. Well, that state at the top of the list in the preceding table should have been your first clue. Also, consider that the nature of a local CPA firm is to prepare itemized tax returns much more frequently than the national average, and that those returns have a far greater likelihood of having an AMT liability than a standard deduction return.

Here are my firm's statistics for 2005 income tax returns completed through April 17, 2006:

Number of completed returns	2,731
Average total income	$84,975
Number of returns with itemized deductions	1,661 (60.8%)
Number of returns with AMT liability	221 (8.09%)
Total amount of additional AMT tax paid (1)	$695,712
Average AMT paid per taxpayer (1)	$3,479

(I) I stratified my database here to take out the top ten and bottom ten affected taxpayers so as not to skew the average by returns that may have had some aberration creating the AMT. Also, note that sometimes when we prepare a return that has an AMT liability, we will not add additional deductions (such as unreimbursed job expenses) which while reducing the regular income tax, only force a greater AMT addback to keep the return at the same total liability (thus, the effect that the average AMT paid is probably low if I put every possible regular income tax deduction on the return).

If we can agree that my sample size of completed returns is large enough to draw comparison with the national average (and since I'm the one at the keyboard, I'll take that as a yes), what conclusions, if any, can we draw from my results?

First, if you are a family of four and live in a high-income tax and property tax state (like New Jersey), you are the poster children for the AMT. You are two to three times more likely than the national average to get caught up in the AMT, and need to do your tax planning around existing in the AMT world and forget about the regular income tax world.

Second, the AMT is not equitably distributed across the country. Making your home in a high cost-of-living state (like New Jersey, New York, or California) will make you much more likely to be hit with the AMT as your income needs to be greater than in lower cost-of-living states just to meet the demands of your living expenses. In my practice (which also handles a number of New York returns), we see this frequently as evidenced by the average income per return as shown above. We continually face the age-old question with our clients of "But where did it all go?" In fact, returning to my 2,731 completed returns, only 30% had interest income or dividend income greater than $1,500 last year. When the national savings rate is practically 0%, I can attest that my client base is pretty average in that regard.

• • •

Coming back to the premise of the book, adopting the alternative minimum tax now, it's time to strip away some of the fundamental flaws in the AMT system so that we can move to an overall total tax system (one world with no evil parallel tax universes) that is less complex and more fair on a national scale skewing the tax burden more towards the upper class and away from the middle class. To accomplish this and retain overall revenue neutrality at the same time is the goal.

Let's get to the plan (man, I hope the payoff for reading this chapter was worth it)!

Simplicity and Fairness, Part 1

If the conceptual framework of the AMT is so simple, why can't the mechanics be simplified as well? We'll examine that issue as we tackle the first part of my plan to simplify the existing AMT.

To that end, we are going to take a look at IRS Form 6251, Alternative Minimum Tax – Individuals, a copy of which (2005 version) is reproduced on the following page.

In Part I, we have 28 lines of items with line 1 being our starting point (regular taxable income before the deduction for personal exemptions) and line 28 being the end point of the calculation of Alternative Minimum Taxable Income. As a quick aside, did you ever wonder why they started with regular taxable income before exemptions and not just regular taxable income? I always figured that this was just another "Congress thinks we're too dumb to notice" decision. If you don't have to addback the exemptions yourself and don't realize what they're up to, it's one less thing to be pissed off about.

Okay, back to simplifying the AMT. How do we take the other 26 lines of AMT-possible adjustments and develop a model that is light years simpler than what exists today?

First of all, we are going to keep (conceptually) four items:

- Line 3: Taxes from Schedule A
- Line 5: Miscellaneous deductions from Schedule A
- Line 6: Itemized Deduction Limitation
- Line 7: Tax Refund from Form 1040, Line 10 or 21

Lines 3, 5, and 7 all fit our framework of only allowing interest and charity deductions, noting that the Form 1040, Line 10 addback of state tax refunds would no longer be applicable under the tax benefit rule concept

Form **6251**
(Rev January 2006)
Department of the Treasury
Internal Revenue Service (99)

Alternative Minimum Tax — Individuals

► See separate instructions.
► Attach to Form 1040 or Form 1040NR.

OMB No. 1545-0074

2005

Attachment Sequence No. **32**

Name(s) shown on Form 1040

Your social security number

Part I Alternative Minimum Taxable Income (See instructions for how to complete each line.)

1. If filing Schedule A (Form 1040), enter the amount from Form 1040, line 41 (minus any amount on Form 8914, line 2), and go to line 2. Otherwise, enter the amount from Form 1040, line 38 (minus any amount on Form 8914, line 2), and go to line 7. (If less than zero, enter as a negative amount.) **1**
2. Medical and dental. Enter the **smaller** of Schedule A (Form 1040), line 4 **or** 2-1/2% of Form 1040, line 38 ... **2**
3. Taxes from Schedule A (Form 1040), line 9 .... **3**
4. Enter the home mortgage interest adjustment, if any, from line 6 of the worksheet in the instructions **4**
5. Miscellaneous deductions from Schedule A (Form 1040), line 26 .... **5**
6. If Form 1040, line 38, is over $145,950 (over $72,975 if married filing separately), enter the amount from line 9 of the **Itemized Deductions Worksheet** in the Instructions for Schedules A and B (Form 1040) **6**
7. Tax refund from Form 1040, line 10 or line 21 .... **7**
8. Investment interest expense (difference between regular tax and AMT) **8**
9. Depletion (difference between regular tax and AMT) **9**
10. Net operating loss deduction from Form 1040, line 21. Enter as a positive amount **10**
11. Interest from specified private activity bonds exempt from the regular tax **11**
12. Qualified small business stock (7% of gain excluded under section 1202) **12**
13. Exercise of incentive stock options (excess of AMT income over regular tax income) **13**
14. Estates and trusts (amount from Schedule K-1 (Form 1041), box 12, Code A) **14**
15. Electing large partnerships (amount from Schedule K-1 (Form 1065-B), box 6) **15**
16. Disposition of property (difference between AMT and regular tax gain or loss) **16**
17. Depreciation on assets placed in service after 1986 (difference between regular tax and AMT) **17**
18. Passive activities (difference between AMT and regular tax income or loss) **18**
19. Loss limitations (difference between AMT and regular tax income or loss) **19**
20. Circulation costs (difference between regular tax and AMT) **20**
21. Long-term contracts (difference between AMT and regular tax income) **21**
22. Mining costs (difference between regular tax and AMT) **22**
23. Research and experimental costs (difference between regular tax and AMT) **23**
24. Income from certain installment sales before January 1, 1987 .... **24**
25. Intangible drilling costs preference **25**
26. Other adjustments, including income-based related adjustments **26**
27. Alternative tax net operating loss deduction **27**
28. **Alternative minimum taxable income.** Combine lines 1 through 27. (If married filing separately and line 28 is more than $191,000, see instructions.) **28**

Part II Alternative Minimum Tax

29. Exemption. (If this form is for a child under age 14, see instructions.)

IF your filing status is ...	AND line 28 is not over ...	THEN enter on line 29 ...
Single or head of household	$112,500	$40,250
Married filing jointly or qualifying widow(er)	150,000	58,000
Married filing separately	75,000	29,000

If line 28 is **over** the amount shown above for your filing status, see instructions. **29**

30. Subtract line 29 from line 28. If zero or less, enter -0- here and on lines 33 and 35 and stop here **30**
31. • If you reported capital gain distributions directly on Form 1040, line 13; you reported qualified dividends on Form 1040, line 9b; **or** you had a gain on both lines 15 and 16 of Schedule D (Form 1040) (as refigured for the AMT, if necessary), complete Part III on page 2 and enter the amount from line 55 here.
    • **All others:** If line 30 is $175,000 or less ($87,500 or less if married filing separately), multiply line 30 by 26% (.26). Otherwise, multiply line 30 by 28% (.28) and subtract $3,500 ($1,750 if married filing separately) from the result. **31**
32. Alternative minimum tax foreign tax credit (see instructions) **32**
33. Tentative minimum tax. Subtract line 32 from line 31 .... **33**
34. Tax from Form 1040, line 44 (minus any tax from Form 4972 and any foreign tax credit from Form 1040, line 47). If you used Schedule J to figure your tax, the amount for line 44 of Form 1040 must be refigured without using Schedule J (see instructions) **34**
35. **Alternative minimum tax.** Subtract line 34 from line 33. If zero or less, enter -0-. Enter here and on Form 1040, line 45 .... **35**

BAA For Paperwork Reduction Act Notice, see separate instructions.   FDIA5312L 01/13/06   Form **6251** (2005) (Rev 1-2006) under section 111 of the Internal Revenue Code (i.e. if I don't get a deduction for something on my return, I don't have to pick up a refund I receive as income on it in a subsequent year).

Now, let's consider the other 22 items:

- Line 2: Medical and Dental
- Line 4: Home Mortgage Interest adjustment
- Line 8: Investment Interest Expense adjustment
- Line 9: Depletion adjustment
- Line 10 and 27: Regular Tax and AMT Net Operating Loss adjustments
- Line 11: Interest from Private Activity Bond adjustment
- Line 12: Qualified Small Business Stock adjustment
- Line 13: Exercise of Incentive Stock Options adjustment
- Line 14: Estates and Trusts adjustment
- Line 15: Electing Large Partnerships adjustment
- Line 16: Disposition of Property adjustment
- Line 17: Depreciation adjustment
- Line 18: Passive Activities adjustment
- Line 19: Loss Limitations adjustment
- Line 20: Circulation Costs adjustment
- Line 21: Long-term Contracts adjustment
- Line 22: Mining Costs adjustment
- Line 23: Research and Experimental Costs adjustment
- Line 24: Income from Certain Installment Sales before January 1, 1987 adjustment
- Line 25: Intangible Drilling Costs Preference adjustment
- Line 26: Other adjustments (?)

DELETE ALL OF THESE ITEMS! There, that was simple, wasn't it?

All right, I know what you're thinking, what about all the money that would be lost by ridding ourselves of these preference items? Wouldn't the super-rich be the only ones to benefit from this change?

I readily concede that revenue would be sacrificed. But I sacrifice it in the name of simplicity! There has to be a cost-benefit somewhere to making this a simpler system, and I choose to make my stand here. And c'mon, look at that list of items again. Most of that stuff is so limited in its application that few people would be affected by their dismissal from the Internal

Revenue Code, and thus, Congress would not have a major revenue drain at the same time.

We'll focus on two items, though, and these are the ones that I tend to see the most in my practice. I specifically exclude the depreciation adjustment, however, as we could devote a whole book to analyzing that system alone. As the two depreciation systems have been more closely aligned over the last few years, though, the cost-benefit of finally merging these systems should be no big deal. The items that I refer to are the private activity bond interest adjustment and the preference adjustment for incentive stock option exercises.

To make the case for disposing of these items, we must at least consider a revenue neutrality concern. Most people would believe that municipal bond ownership (in an amount where the income generated actually makes a real difference in someone's life) and being a person that would have incentive stock options to exercise does not rest with middle-class Americans (and I'll let you work with your own preconceived notion of what constitutes middle class), but rather with the upper class (or the rich or even super rich). Our system must contain a trade-off that will appease the masses.

Before we can get to that, we must address one other AMT topic. In the next chapter, we will simplify the last complex area of the calculation of the AMT tax and deal with AMT's most unfair component: the AMT exemption.

Simplicity and Fairness, Part 2

The AMT exemption is the last determining factor in whether a taxpayer gets caught in the AMT or pays only the regular income tax.

The AMT exemption is merely a flat deduction amount that is determined by a taxpayer's filing status (i.e. single, married filing jointly, etc.) with said amount being subtracted from the AMT income to arrive at AMT taxable income.

As I write this, President Bush has just signed into law the Tax Increase Prevention and Reconciliation Act of 2005. One of the clauses of this Act is a one-year relief provision from having the AMT exemption deductions revert back to their pre-2003 levels which in and of itself would have subjected (by the government's estimate) an additional fifteen million middle-class Americans to paying the AMT tax. In addition, they took the 2005 exemption amounts and increased them slightly for 2006. I (and perhaps, you, too) must question Congress's resolve to deal with tax complexity when they pass tax laws that affect a single year only. Frankly, it's little more than an election year ploy to keep the voters happy (not dissimilar to the timing of President Bush's last major piece of tax legislation passed just a few weeks before the presidential election in 2004), and we should be smart enough to see it for what it is and not part of any long-term solution to how we tax our citizens in this country.

Getting back to the point, if the AMT exemption deduction is just a flat amount, where is the complexity and why is it unfair?

Let's tackle the complexity issue first. What makes the exemption "not simple" is that it isn't truly a flat amount for all filers in the same filing classification. As income increases beyond certain levels, Congress says that you are not entitled to the full amount of the exemption and must begin reducing it by an amount determined by how much your AMT income exceeds their arbitrarily-determined threshold. Anytime you have to deal with a phaseout of a fixed deduction, you are adding a layer of complexity to the Code. And yes, I understand that that's why we have computer programs to calculate our taxes. But, if you can't easily explain how a number on your tax return is determined, then it is too complicated. So get rid of this law. No more phasing out the AMT exemption deduction.

Next, we'll consider the fairness issue. I remind you (again) that I come from a northeast state (New Jersey) and while our average income is amongst the highest in the country, so is our cost of living. Fairness, ultimately, is about value judgments. Everyone has their own judgments, and you may not agree with mine. In the end, though, doesn't an engaging debate depend on different values? How boring life would be if we all agreed on everything. So, here is my idea on how to make the AMT exemption deduction fair for everyone.

There are three things we need to do to the AMT exemption to make it fair:

1. The AMT exemption deduction for those married filing jointly needs to be double that of single filers.

2. The AMT exemption deduction needs to be a higher amount for taxpayers living in higher cost-of-living states and less for taxpayers living in lower cost-of-living states.

3. The AMT exemption deduction needs to be adjusted annually for inflation.

Starting with point #1, I think this is pretty straightforward. Consider back a couple of years ago when solving the marriage penalty was all in vogue. We saw that the regular income tax standard deduction for married taxpayers was not double that of single taxpayers and the regular income tax brackets for married taxpayers were not double that of single taxpayers. What did Congress ultimately do to make the regular income tax system more fair? They doubled the single standard deduction for married filers, and doubled the regular income tax brackets to put everybody on a level playing field.

But how about in the AMT world? No such luck! Two single people living together still get a far greater AMT exemption deduction than if they were married. So married couples are far more likely to get hit with the

AMT than single taxpayers. And as an additional "benefit" for single filers, the AMT tax brackets are exactly the same as married filers which means that two single people (in the AMT) would pay less than their married counterparts. (In this case, necessarily, I recommend halving the bracket break for single filers and not doubling up for marrieds.) Thus, in the interest of fairness, when we adopt the AMT as our "one and only" tax system, we must have an AMT exemption for married filers that is double that of single filers to rid ourselves of the AMT marriage penalty.

For the second point of different AMT exemptions based on where you live, my two debatable points are: "How do you keep it simple?" and "How do you do it fairly?"

As to simplicity, let's compare to the recent resurrection of the sales tax deduction back into the regular income tax code (remember that this deduction was eliminated in the early 1980's). If Congress can develop a table that has a different base sales tax deduction depending on what state you live in, how tough can it be to come up with a table that has a different AMT exemption deduction for each state?

And I wouldn't even suggest that, anyway. I say group the states into five strata and then have just five levels of exemption. Much easier. What if I move during the year? Again, we could make this complex by prorating the exemption over the days you lived in each state or make it easy by using the exemption for the state you live in on December 31st. I vote for the easy way. You could argue that it's not fair if you move from a high cost to a low cost state late in the year (thus, having high income and a low exemption), but as I said earlier, some sacrifices need to be made for simplicity's sake. The needs of the many outweigh the needs of the few or the one (stealing a line from Leonard Nimoy as Mr. Spock in <u>Star Trek II: The Wrath of Khan</u>).

Now, how do we figure out a fair amount for the AMT exemption deduction for each strata? Well, time to put some economists to work. Revisiting our statistics, let's use the cost-of-living index for each state to group them into each strata. Those ten states with the highest cost of living relative to the other forty (plus Washington, D.C.) go into Group 1. The next highest ten states go into Group 2. States 21 to 30 (the middle or base amount states as we'll refer to them) go in Group 3. Group 4 will be for states 31 to 40, and Group 5 will be for the ten states with the lowest statistical cost of living in the country. Based on the 3rd quarter 2005 Composite Cost-of-Living Index, the states would fall into the following groups:

Group 1
Alaska
California
Connecticut
District of Columbia
Hawaii
Massachusetts
Maryland
New Jersey
New York
Rhode Island
Vermont

Group 2
Arizona
Florida
Maine
New Hampshire
Nevada
Oregon
Pennsylvania
Virginia
Washington
Wyoming

Group 3
Colorado
Delaware
Louisiana
Minnesota
Montana
Michigan
North Carolina
New Mexico
Ohio
Wisconsin

<u>Group 4</u>
Alabama
Georgia
Iowa
Idaho
Illinois
Indiana
South Carolina
South Dakota
Utah
West Virginia

<u>Group 5</u>
Arkansas
Kansas
Kentucky
Missouri
Mississippi
North Dakota
Nebraska
Oklahoma
Tennessee
Texas

Once we determine the base AMT exemption deductions for single taxpayers (which will also include head of household and married filing separate taxpayers) and married filing jointly taxpayers (including qualified widows/widowers), we will assign that amount to the Group 3 states. The Group 2 states will get 110% of the base amount, and the Group 1 states will get 120% of the base amount. In Group 4, they will use as their exemption 90% of the base amount, and the Group 5 states will use 80% of the base amount. Thus, in terms of simplicity, this is pretty easy. All we have to do is come up with one number and everything else falls right into place.

Okay then, what is the number and who should determine it?

We need to consider the impact of our choices here. Basically, my model moves some of the tax burden in this country from married taxpayers to single taxpayers, and it moves some of the tax burden from the high cost- of-living states (primarily on the East and West Coasts) to the lower cost-of- living states (principally middle America). The development of the AMT exemption deduction should be predicated on swinging some of the tax burden away from the middle-class married taxpayers on the East and West Coasts and to the upper-class single and married taxpayers in middle America. For too long, tax benefits have been skewed against those with high incomes (who tend to also live in high cost-of-living states) to those who enjoy a higher standard of living in a low-cost state. The availability of tax benefits like the child tax credit and education credits (as well as a multitude of other items) are dependent on the calculation of adjusted gross income. Thus, someone considered middle-class in a place like New Jersey would still have a high adjusted gross income but not be able to receive many benefits that a comparable middle class person in a place like Nebraska could. But this model is not a middle-class tax for middle America. It is a redistribution of the tax to wealthy middle America who have higher standards of living on lower comparable income than their East and West Coast brethren. I quite fervently believe that this model, at worst, would not change the amount of taxes a middle-class middle America family would pay. At best, these families would see a reduction in their income tax burden right along with the middle-class taxpayers in the higher cost-of- living states.

As to determining the particular starting AMT exemption number, you and I, as citizens, pay a group of people who work for an organization called the Government Accountability Office (GAO), who should be responsible for developing the number. Their charge should be, using the accumulated tax data of the last several years, to see what amount would result in relative revenue neutrality for the federal government.

Is that a copout? You thought I knew the number? Do you feel let down?

Not to worry, I have a starting number in mind. But unlike Steve Forbes in the mid-1990's, I'm not running for president, so I don't have to tell you. Just kidding. Actually, during last tax season (preparing 2005 tax returns), I was doing a very unscientific, informal study of those people who were paying the AMT and at what exemption amount would the results have been fairly neutral between their regular income tax and the AMT tax. The problem many of my clients ran into was the AMT exemption phaseout. If the exemption was not phased out, while most would still have paid some AMT (in the hundreds of dollars as opposed to thousands) it would have been greatly reduced.

Thus, thinking about living in a Group 1 state (New Jersey), without an AMT exemption phaseout, married taxpayers would have paid approximately the same regular income tax as AMT tax using an exemption amount of $58,000 (2005's base amount). However, if we set the number at that level going forward, I believe overall tax revenue would be negatively impacted when extrapolated over both itemizers and standard deduction filers. As a result, I'm going to make the determination to reduce the exemption by $10,000 to $48,000, a level where I feel revenue neutrality could be more realistically achieved.

Therefore, by picking $48,000 as the Group 1 AMT exemption, we can work backwards to the AMT exemption deduction for marrieds in a Group 3 base state. Doing the (simple) math, the Group 3 AMT exemption for married filers would be $40,000 ($48,000 divided by 120%).

This sets the stage now for everything else. Singles in Group 3 states would get a $20,000 AMT exemption deduction at one-half the married rate with the other groups breaking down as follows:

AMT EXEMPTION DEDUCTION

	Married Filing Joint, & Qualified Widow (er)	Single, Head of HH, & Married Filing Separate
Group 1	$48,000	$24,000
Group 2	$44,000	$22,000
Group 3	$40,000	$20,000
Group 4	$36,000	$18,000
Group 5	$32,000	$16,000

Finally, to point #3, the base AMT exemption deduction amounts for married and single filers must be indexed annually for the national cost-of-living increase. Failure to do so is tantamount to an annual tax increase.

• • •

Well, that is the plan. But how is Congress going to sell this to the masses?
Read on MacDuff, we're almost to the finish line.

It's the Bureaucracy, Dummy!

How in the world is Congress ever going to be able to sell America on abandoning the regular income tax and adopting the AMT? If you're like all my clients, you hate the AMT. The mere suggestion that the AMT be "the" tax system would lead you to join a taxpayer revolt and vote against any politician backing such a proposal.

So listen up Congress. I'll give you the blueprint for achieving tax simplicity, fairness, and revenue neutrality all without alienating your core constituency – middle-class America.

First, you must sell to America that you're serious about tax simplification. Your top priority is to **REPEAL THE AMT!**

Second, in the interest of tax fairness, you have to make a few changes to the regular income tax code. To that end, you will do the following:

- Give a brand new, big exemption amount to both single and married taxpayers to replace the deductions for exemptions; and for long-form filers (itemizers), to replace the write-offs for taxes and miscellaneous itemized deductions (i.e. job-related deductions, tax prep fees, etc.). Standard deduction filers (remember, 70% of all filers) would be unaffected while itemizers would still be able to deduct medical costs (subject to a new, lower 5% of AGI threshold), interest (home mortgage and investment interest subject to their current regular income tax restrictions), charitable contributions, casualty and theft losses (subject to current restrictions), and gambling losses to extent of winnings (along with a few other pre-existing miscellaneous deductions not subject to the AGI limitation).

- For taxpayers in higher cost-of-living states than those ten states with the lowest relative cost of living, their exemptions will be scaled higher to account for this, and the amount will be determined by the GAO (not Congress or the IRS), and will be adjusted annually for inflation.

- To further simplify the tax code, the regular income tax brackets will be compressed from five to two: 26% on the first $175,000 of income for marrieds and 28% over that amount. Singles, heads of household, and marrieds filing separate would pay 26% on the first $87,500 and 28% over that amount.

- All tax credits (both refundable and nonrefundable) will be maintained as is.

- Finally, upon passage of the above changes to the Internal Revenue Code, all AMT provisions will be repealed!

I personally envision dancing in the streets when people hear that last part. You, dear reader, and I will realize, of course, that what has been accomplished has been the remaking of the regular income tax code into the AMT and then changing the name back (kind of like how SBC Communications took over AT&T).

Naturally, people may feel uneasy trying to figure out their individual savings or costs with these changes. Congress, you will have to work hard to assure the lower and middle-class taxpayers that they will pay no more than what they are paying now, will likely pay less and will have a simpler time computing their federal taxes. But to show you're serious about reducing their taxes and to ensure a truly revenue-neutral overall change to the tax system, you are going to make one more change to make sure the rich pay their fair share of taxes.

Congress, you must pass a law that caps the preference rate of tax on qualified dividends at $2,000 per year for married taxpayers and $1,000 per year for singles. Qualified dividends in excess of those amounts will be taxed again as ordinary income.

By doing this, wealthy stock owners/taxpayers will pay more in taxes and that should make up for any revenue shortfall for getting rid of the other AMT preference items, notably private activity bond interest and incentive stock option exercise income.

If things work out well, we could even generate a budget surplus to help pay down some of our government debt. Further, to encourage corporations to continue paying (or even increasing) their dividends, Congress should offer a partial corporate income tax deduction for dividend payouts.

There you go, Congress. It's a combination sales job/snow job. Most people will never realize what's happened, but they should be happier taxpayers because they'll be convinced that our system of taxation is now simpler and fairer.

All we have to do to make this a reality is to not get bogged down in the bureaucracy and **ADOPT THE AMT NOW!**

Afterword

At this stage, we've simplified and made fairer the income tax system in the United States for most taxpayers. However, two of the vexing problems still remaining are dealing with individuals who could be claimed as a dependent by someone else, and for some of them, the kiddie tax.

In the Tax Increase Prevention and Reconciliation Act of 2005, Congress (as a revenue offset measure) increased the age by which the kiddie tax would apply from those under age fourteen to those under age eighteen. In my tax model the difference between the child's rate and that of their parent(s) is negligible (2% at worst if the parent(s) is in the 28% tax bracket), so we really don't need a special kiddie tax. The problem that becomes evident is not a tax bracket savings between generations, but rather the AMT exemption for singles.

If individuals who can be claimed as dependents were given the full amount of an AMT single exemption, it would create a huge incentive (and a major inequity) for wealthy taxpayers to transfer assets and income to those dependents (principally, their kids). Thus, we must add a provision to our model for that circumstance and take away the base AMT single exemption for dependents.

We do, however, need to provide a "dependent" AMT exemption to account for the difference in tax brackets that someone who could be claimed as a dependent by another person would face. Currently, some or all of their income would be taxed at just 10%. Under the new model that same income would now be taxed at 26%. To deal with this inequity, we must look at the two groups of people who can be claimed as dependents by others: those people under age eighteen, and those ages eighteen and older.

The under age eighteen group is our kiddie tax group, and as they only achieve a relatively small benefit in the current 10% regular income tax bracket, they will only need a small "dependent" AMT exemption to make this law (mostly) revenue neutral for them. By providing them an AMT exemption of one-and-one-half percent (1.5%) of the AMT single exemption for their state, the net plus/minus in their income tax would be nominal.

For the age eighteen and older group, if they have income greater than the standard deduction for a single person, it is generally a result of working a part-time job, and they should not be penalized for working by paying taxes at the higher income tax rate without a greater "dependent" AMT exemption than the under eighteen group. For them, I propose using an AMT exemption of seven-and-one-half percent (7.5%) of the AMT single exemption for their state.

Necessarily, it is harder to achieve revenue neutrality for this group as there is a breakpoint of income where below that level, the dependent would pay less tax than under current regular income tax law and more above that level. As stated in earlier chapters, though, certain sacrifices need to be made for simplicity's sake, and tying a "dependent" AMT exemption to the base AMT exemption avoids the problem of having to revisit this issue on a periodic basis.

• • •

As my last word (of this Afterword), I offer up "epistemology." Epistemology is the study of knowledge, and in a sense, we are all students with no graduation date. If we break down knowledge into three categories, I'll provide you my final thoughts and hopes for this book.

First, as to knowledge, there are things that you really know (i.e. I know a lot about taxes and accounting, I know the rules of football, etc.); next, there are things you've heard about, but don't really know (i.e. I've heard of brain surgery, but I don't know how to do it); and finally, there are things that you don't know, and you don't even know that you don't know them. My goal (as an ardent student of epistemology) is to try to learn more about things that I have only a minimal awareness of, and to expose myself to new ideas and concepts that I have no current awareness of with the result of moving that idea out of the "don't know" column and into the "at least I've heard of it" column in my brain.

And on the flip side, as a teacher (and we all teach something to someone in the course of our lives), I hope that I've taken my ideas and concepts and done the same for you.

Let the debate begin.

Acknowledgments

It was great fun writing this book and I hope you enjoyed my perspective on our system of federal taxation. Among those I would like to thank include my wife, Laura, and our daughters, Melissa and Megan. You are my toughest critics, but also my greatest supporters. My heartfelt thanks in helping make this book a reality. Also, for my business partner, Tom Colletti, and our accounting staff, thanks for sharing your insights and experiences for me to draw upon when developing my ideas.

Finally, there are two writers/commentators who have helped shape my writing style and while I know neither one personally, I'd like to mention them. First, Stephen King, whose <u>Dark Tower</u> books are not so much reading as feeling you are sitting on the back porch being told a story. I tried to emulate his easy going, let's-have-a-chat feel, and if I was one-tenth as successful as he is, I know I will have accomplished something. Second, Jon Stewart, whose <u>America: The Book</u> was consistently laugh-out-loud funny and had such a sharp edge. I think his wit and sensibility are to be admired, and for those who view our government's actions with a cynical eye, <u>The Daily Show</u> is a daily "must watch."